THE COFFEE SHOP:

LIFE CHALLENGES AND OPPORTUNITIES

BY

AWUDU QUAN

The Coffee Shop: Life Challenges and Opportunities

Copyright © 2021 by Awudu Quan
Cover design and edits by Candace Paul

All rights reserved. No part of this publication may be reproduced, distributed, or transmitted in any form or by any means, including photocopying, recording, or other electronic or mechanical methods, without the prior written permission of the author, except in the case of brief quotations embodied in critical reviews and certain other noncommercial uses permitted by copyright law. For permission requests, write to the publisher addressed "Attention: Publisher" at the email address below.

ISBN: 978-1-7333675-8-5

Ordering Information:
Quantity sales. Special discounts are available on quantity purchases by churches, associations, and others. For details, contact the author at the address below.
Orders by U.S. trade bookstores and wholesalers. Please email admin@aknowingspirit.com.

Dedication

Nana Zachariah Appiah (Father), Abenaa Fati Yeboaa (Mother), my wife Chen Wen and my daughter Yeboaa Quan for their inspiration.

Contents

CHAPTER 1
INTRODUCTION.................................. 4

CHAPTER 2
COMPLAINTS ABOUT LIFE
CHALLENGES...................................... 9

CHAPTER 3
THE TASTE OF LIFE CHALLENGES....... 16

CHAPTER 4
IN THE COFFEE SHOP 19

CHAPTER 5
GENERAL ADVICE 28

ACKNOWLEDGEMENTS..................... 32

CHAPTER 1
Introduction

This book is generally about life. The first chapter is more of an overview of what to expect, from a book like this, while the second chapter delves more into the challenges most of us face. This book will explore how people approach challenges in life. You will learn about the common complaints many tend to have (you have probably hear most of them). Then, you will be introduced to three very different people in the pursuit of success. After reading the profiles of these individuals, you must determine which one is nearest to you? Next you must decide of these, whose attitude and outlook would eventually lead to success?

Have you ever tasted raw coffee? If not, the third chapter compares life's challenges to the taste of raw coffee. For instance, some who have come to strongly dislike coffee, typically remember the first taste of raw coffee without the sweeteners or the cream. They think that coffee tastes bitter - and for that matter, they never want to bother themselves again to have a second taste. They completely give up on coffee, and refuse to try it again. In a way, this is exactly how many people approach life. They perceive challenges as bitter and very unpleasant.

When they start working toward their goals - just like that first sip of raw coffee, they are immediately confronted with challenges that are bitter and unpleasant. As a result, they are unable to withstand the pressure, and they quit.

The chapter discusses further how the bitterness of coffee can be masked, by adding some flavors to enhance the taste. There are even some that now enjoy the taste of raw coffee just as it is. However, this *new* outlook is only reserved for those that never gave up after their first bad experience with coffee. The same could be said about life's challenges.

We are the architects of our own life. So often we forget that with constant perseverance we shall be able to accomplish our goals.

"Oh, you who believe! Persevere in patience and constancy. Vie in such perseverance, strengthen each other, and be pious, that you may prosper (Quran, 3:200)". According to the Bible in James 1:2-4, "Count it all joy, my brothers, when you meet trials of various kinds, for you know that the testing of your faith produces steadfastness. And let steadfastness have its full effect, that you may be perfect and complete, lacking in nothing."

Surprisingly, everybody wants to be successful, but not everyone who is able to withstand challenges in life succeeds.

The fourth chapter talks about the opportunities in the coffee shop. Do you know what the coffee shop has become? It is an important business serving many purposes well beyond coffee. The chapter begins with a story of a person who wanted to become an entrepreneur and along the line failed several times pursuing his dream.

Initially, he thought that it was inadequate capital that led to his failures, but later he was able to identify the real cause of his numerous failures, and it wasn't money. He identified that it was lack of good managerial skills and knowledge on his part that brought about his failures. And as a result of that, he lost the little capital he had invested. All his workers left because he could not afford to pay their salaries. Eventually, he was evicted from his office unable to pay the office rent. Nevertheless, he was determined to make his vision come true. However, he did not know how to start again without any capital.

One day he went to the coffee shop for a hot cup of coffee, but found much more. There, in the coffee shop, he discovered that there was more than cheerful baristas and a variety of coffee blends. There were opportunities!

The coffee shop is the perfect place for short business discussions, meetings, and long study hours among others.

During is time in the coffee shop, he spotted someone using the space we normally run in and out of, like a temporal office. This man who not too long ago was down on his luck, suddenly became inspired. He took note, and began to use the coffee shop as his office and saved a bunch of money on rent.

While using the coffee shop as a makeshift office he was able to raise enough money to breathe new life into his vision. What's more, he studied for his Masters in Business Administration (MBA) online in that same coffee shop. For the price of a cup of coffee and a few hours each day, this man was able to regroup and learn more about business - after numerous failures. This new way of looking at a place he had always been, turned into a lasting solution for constant challenges.

The fifth chapter is the last chapter. In those pages, I offer general advice about how to stay strong when facing what seems like endless challenges. No matter how hard life gets, you need to be courageous and confront those challenges head on. There is a quote I love: "Courage is one step ahead of fear."

Chapter five depicts the life of a man who was confronted with many challenges (he lost his job, around the same time his wife had delivered thier first born. He opened several letters marked, "PAST DUE", in addition to threatening calls for eviction.)

Sometimes, the challenges we endure are there to keep us strong. With hard work, that man was able to overcome every challenge he had the courage to confront, and learned that the world has opportunities for everyone. First, we must realized that some opportunities appear to us as challenges until we are strong enough to grasp them. Those who cannot manage challenges, will not be able to manage success

Your ability to manage challenges determine your success or failure.

CHAPTER 2
Complaints About Life Challenges

Today, I came across a belief. A belief I think is not for everyone. It is a belief in a struggle. The struggle for life. This struggle I have endured throughout my life's journey. Surprisingly, I have become the man of a struggle. That is my new identity.

It is an identity I never expected, but in a way, life ordained me.

Today, I came across another belief. A belief I think is destiny. The destiny of the struggle. It seems anything I do is beaten by the wind. Chickens tend to follow the wind. It appears that they move to and fro without any goal in mind. But that is not me. I have a specific purpose for my life.

So why then do I experience so much suffering with nothing to show for it? And today, I have seen real suffering. Believe me, suffering is not for everyone.

I always reflect on the words of Pablo Picasso, "Everything you can imagine is real and in my imagination, I always see my life achievements but in reality, I see them not."

Or maybe am I to apply what Albert

Einstein said, "Logic would get you from A to B. Imagination would take you everywhere."

Such is what life has presented to me. Today, I saw what I didn't expect to see and believed what I planned not to believe. I took more deep breaths than what I normally do. I pulled all my strength into work like a Trojan because Maya Angelou said that, "Nothing would work unless you do."

Yet, it appears life is moving in a direction, not of my choosing. Everyday, I see richness around me - and as walk by, life has decided to bring to me struggle. Is it destiny? I look around at the order of the natural world and lament that I am in great pain with life's challenges.

It is ironic. I could see success from afar, yet near I could see it not. I am following the rubric of the other successful people around me. I am following the steps the majority of them did, yet I am still not succeeding.

Something must be wrong - but not my fault. Success, as they say, is the blessing of hard work. I am working just as hard. So, where is my blessing? This is beyond my understanding.

Nonetheless, I know, that in order to get farm produce, a farmer must prepare the land. He must also plant the seeds. However, seeds do not germinate by the sweat of the farmer's brow, it is the glory of nature that allows that process. Then, once the seeds finally start to grow, the farmer receives glory from his work.

The process is beautiful indeed. The rain falls and the soil provides fertility for the seeds. The germinated seeds grow to bear flowers. Then the sweat of the farmer - plowing, picking, and separating, feeds many mouths. Oh, nature!

I want to be a useful creature to others. Let my presence count and be beneficial to others. As your son, I have prepared my land, planted my seeds. Bestow your glory on me for my germination.

*****

An old man I met in search of life's success told me, "Life is being alive." He eyed me carefully before he spoke. Then with a foreboding tone, the old man said, "Be prepared to struggle more than others in life."

I felt all the weight of his words fall upon me. His prophecy deeply saddened me. I was already struggling…I was going to struggle more?! He was right. Life had never danced to my tune. Was I cursed or what?

I figured I may be the only person in this world that struggles. Nothing of mine had been successful. The old man interrupted my thought and continued - although I hoped he wouldn't.

"My son, in life you are *always* a seed, yet to be germinated. It's simple, you either survive germination or you rot."

Straight-faced, I waited for him to finish his thought.

"Is that it?"

The old man chuckled, "In as much as you are alive, you either succeed or fail."

He held his arms behind his back looking expectantly at the sky.

"Rain falls every year and the sun shines everyday. Decide which favors your germination."

I folded my arms and considered his words. I thought to myself, won't I need both? As if the old man felt my confusion he said, "Always remember that not all trees grow well in every season. Some need more water to grow and some need more sun."

***

In achieving success and greatness in life, there are three types of people you meet.

The first type are the ones who seem to be born great. These people might have physical features that are considered very attractive, an abundance of charm, or innate talent, that sets them apart from others. Wherever these people find themselves, they will germinate, grow, and bear flowers. For them, whether winter or summer, they are able to thrive in every situation. But in life, these people are rare.

The second group are those in which

greatness is bestowed on them. They are not seeding or awaiting germination, but rather they are already ripe fruit. They always enjoy the greatness of others. In life, such people do not have to struggle, nor face many challenges, because the path has been set by the successful ones that came before them. These people are typically born into the comforts of a wealthy family.

Last, the third group are those that are neither born great, nor whose path was paved by the greatness of their predecessors. These are the ones who strive to achieve greatness for themselves.

They are those who believe in hard work and work like a trojan to achieve success. For them, there is no substitute for hard work if you want to become successful in life.

Most people fall into the third group because of circumstance. They can neither rely on looks or wealth to become successful. Their only option for success is hard work. To achieve greatness, always compare yourself to these three groups and choose the one that closely mirrors your circumstance. Doing this self check will help you determine your path to success.

Do not look down upon yourself because you have not been successful in what you are doing. But rather always believe that one day you will be successful.

Interestingly, you are not alone deep inside

the soil struggling to germinate - meaning you are not the only person struggling to succeed. Remember, those who truly succeed, see challenges in life as opportunities for growth.

Life is knocking at your door. You either open it or not. George Bernard Shaw, Irish playwright and political activist, once said, "Life isn't about finding yourself. Life is about creating yourself."

All of us experience major and minor life challenges. However, how we handle these struggles on a daily basis determine our physical and mental well-being.

"Do not dwell in the past, do not dream of the future, concentrate on the present moment," Buddha said. Many people tend to forget that what they do every day is a culmination of their past and future. If this is the case, why not concentrate on the things that better yourself every day?

It takes a single occurrence to convince us that we have no control over our conditions. From time to time, these challenges consume us with guilt, panic, and chronic fatigue. The predicaments we find ourselves in can add pressure from every side - threatening to smash us.

Coincidentally, all challenges in life directly correlate to the clarity of our goals. If only we could find some assurance that there is a reason for the difficulties we face. We tend to search for meaning in tragedy. We question our purpose and search for hope for the future. We lament, "Oh, why me God? And why this time? When will I be blessed?"

The good news is that challenges in life enable us to examine ourselves to identify and learn where we excel and where we can improve. But when we are hit with challenges in life, initially, we attempt to escape. Some people develop addictions to alcohol or drugs. Others find themselves so devastated they contemplate suicide, or worse, carry it out.

My friend and his parents were victims of emotional and verbal abuse. They struggled with self-worth. Eventually, they discovered a way to keep their heart and mind in tact. They found peace and joy by using kind words to bring positive thinking such as hope and healing to themselves, not as verbal weapons.

Zig Ziglar, an author and motivational speaker, once wrote, "Positive thinking would let you do everything better than negative thinking would." Walter Scott, Scottish novelist and poet, had a similar outlook. "For success, attitude is equally important as ability," Scott said. This implies that our attitude towards the challenges we face is essential to making the biggest difference in our circumstances.

CHAPTER 3
The Taste of Life Challenges

Challenges in life for many people is like the taste of raw coffee. The first time, the taste of coffee can be bitter. That first experience can make people become coffee haters.

Fortunately, those who try it again learn to like coffee because they discover ways to enhance the taste. They learn that they can add sweeteners, milk, or creme to make the taste less bitter. In a way, this is how many people perceive life. Which one of them are you? Indulge me for a moment as I compare coffee to our understanding of success.

• *Do you hate coffee just because of its raw taste?* Are you the type of person that hates everything about the challenges that are presented in life?

• *Do you realize that the bitterness of coffee can be masked with milk and sugar?* Are you the type of person that can see the value in your present challenge. For instance, find the sweet parts?

• *Do you realize that coffee naturally has blends that make it taste good when you know them?* Are you a person that has learned to welcome challenges, because you know that challenges are just part of life?

Many people are not able to reach their goals and aspirations in life because they could not survive the challenges the faced. But this does not have to be the outcome you experience. If we want to enjoy life and be more effective in it, we should orient ourselves toward facing life challenges whichever way they present themselves to us. Once we are able to develop that strong mentality and a positive attitude toward life, we could deal with life more effectively. Therefore, what was initially challenging and foreign to us would simply become familiar. As a result, life would then become more manageable and easier to endure.

Often, because of the challenges we face, everything can become confusing. Ultimately, we lose interest in anything and become dissatisfied rather quickly with the direction life, but find ourselves at a loss for how to change its present course.

No matter what the challenges, we need to manage our feelings in order to find satisfaction, meaning, and pleasure in life. Doing this simple action (managing feelings) helps us to stay strong psychologically. That way we can pursue the life we want. Do not forget, that with persistence, many first-time coffee takers have developed a love for coffee and have identified ways to change its bitter taste in order to suit their personal preferences.

Life is a learning process and there will always be peculiar challenges. We must constantly be in learning mode. No one gets it "right" all the time. However, our kind-hearted attitude toward our circumstances and ourselves, can only help us stay on course.

Albert Camus, French philosopher and Nobel Prize winner wrote:

"You cannot create an experience. You must undergo it."

We learn best from experience. We learn that we can both succeed and recover from failure. This is because, "The reward of suffering is experience," Harry S. Truman said.

We so often count our troubles instead of counting our blessings. However, this attitude undermines our ability to draw from all the good we have been given. We fail to understand that at its core, life is a gift.

Changing your perspective could make all the difference. Recognizing the good and receiving it with gratitude is a recipe for emotional health and well-being. This attitude increases the possibility that we could make use of the good we have been given and even use it to cope with the difficulties that we inevitably inherit.

CHAPTER 4
In the Coffee Shop

Every day people wake with ideas and plans to pursue their life goals. Nevertheless, even with such grand ideas and well laid plans, not everyone is able to achieve their intended goals. Some give up on the process, and some end up settling on anything that will provide a daily meal. In the midst of those that fail and those that settle, there are still those that achieve their goals. Where do you belong?

Like everyone, my friend also had a vision for his life. He dreamed of becoming an entrepreneur. He decided to go full speed ahead and pursue his entrepreneurial vision. It wasn't long before he was able to establish his first business. Still, he failed several times along the line.

Initially, he thought it was a result of inadequate capital which led to the collapse of the business. In those times, he did not have enough capital to sustain his workers. Worst of all, he ended up losing his office apartment because he could not afford to pay the office rent.

Later, he realized that not having enough capital was just a minor contributor to his various failures. Most small businesses perform abysmally - not because they have little money, instead it is the inability to *manage* the little money they have to grow. That was the situation my friend found himself in.

He had the burning desire to become an entrepreneur and was able to establish a business to that effect. He even believed he would be able to manage the business by himself. Many small business owners have the same notion: Once they open a business, they will manage it. However, many of them may not have adequate managerial skills.

In the beginning, my friend thought the business model he had would generate enough capital quickly. But that didn't happen. All the workers stopped working, and the landlord evicted him from his apartment. All of this sent my friend spiraling down a pit of confusion and despair. He found himself at a crossroads: Give up on his vision and find something to make ends meet, or continue pursuing his entrepreneurial vision of which he had already lost so much?

There were many ideas and plans that came to him. Those thoughts pushed him to contact many people from all around the cardinal points for their advice about what he should do. Many of them spoke from personal life experiences to advise him. The culmination of their advice to him was: 1) to stay focused, and 2) that he would only be considered a "failure" if he gives up.

The sleepless nights were becoming more frequent. One particular night, as he contemplated the many ways he could possibly resurrect his vision, the words of inventor, Thomas A. Edson flashed in his mind. "I have not failed, I have just found 10,000 ways that won't work." Edson said.

He thought about this particular quote for hours and applied it to his own life. The ways he was approaching his business did not work. The answer was not to give up, but instead to find the right way. He decided then, no matter how hard it would be for him to pursue his vision, he would not give up.

The stark reality of his circumstances was setting in. Although he could reflect on all the motivational quotes in the world, they still would not help him pin-point his next move.

My friend was not alone. This very situation happens to many people. Regardless of the number of lectures they attend or the number of motivational quotes they can remember, they get stuck and cannot devise a new strategy in order to bounce back. As a result, they give up.

My friend nearly quit too. I am sure that as you read this, there is something in your life - maybe in academics or in your career, that you considered quitting. But if it is something your really want, this should not be an option for you. You need to persevere and go after it.

Make a list of all your challenges and check which is the most concerning one and attend to it first.

Sometimes, you do not need to resolve all your problems before you can move forward with your life. In the case of my friend, he erroneously believed that his biggest challenge was not having enough money, but in fact, it was not. This happens to many people.

Ironically, people are unable to identify their main problem. They don't give it much attention in order to resolve it, but rather give it attention in order to complain. They falsely believe that they are not as lucky as others. They cite people they know personally who have become successful, or those that they have heard or watched on television sharing their personal stories of success. They use these stories to justify that these people are "lucky" - not that their success was a result of hard work.

At the point when he initially failed, he also had the same mindset. But the truth of the matter is that many people have not been able to identify their main problem. They have no clue why they failed, keep failing, or related to business, why their businesses are not performing up to its targeted goals.

As I have indicated in the previous chapter,

yes, some people are born lucky. They have gotten support, but that is not a yardstick to dwell on, or a reason to quit or give up on your path. In the pursuit of achieving life goals, some people are born great, greatness is bestowed on others, and the rest have to work hard in order to achieve greatness for themselves.

Identify which one defines you. And don't make unnecessary comparisons to discourage yourself.

For my friend to resurrect his entrepreneurial vision, he decided to work from home. Unfortunately, that idea did not work for him either. He was living in a compound house, in a shared room with his siblings. He expressed to them that he wanted to use the room as an office space. At first, he could not persuade them to give him the space and time to work on his vision. When he finally convinced them, the issue of privacy became an ongoing problem which led to several misunderstandings. He could not continue to use the place as an office.

When this happened, he began to have doubts again. Maybe he was not destined to succeed. If you find yourself in a situation like this right now, you do not need to worry at all. Challenges are part of our life, and you should know that you are not the first person and would not be the last person to encounter difficulties pursuing your vision.

The truth is that all the successful people you wish to be also went through challenges to acquire their wealth, and are still going through challenges to maintain their acquired wealth. If you continue to persevere, at all costs, one day you will be successful and people will hear your success story and wish to be like you.

To recap, my friend had no money to rent an office, nor any money to hire workers. He could not operate from home either. So how did he overcome these challenges?

As an entrepreneur, you must always have your eyes open for opportunities around you. This will keep you one step ahead of everyone else.

One day he went to a coffee shop to get a cup of coffee. Have you noticed that the coffee shop has morphed into a place that serves many purposes? When he arrived at the coffee shop, he sat there for some time, pondering on ways he could bounce back from the set back.

On that first day, he left the coffee shop without being able to make any rational decision about his vision. He also had not identified any opportunities in the coffee shop. Three days later, he went back, and while he was sitting there sipping his coffee, his attention was divided. At one point, he was curious about all the conversations happening inside, while at the same he thought about his problems. He became so interested in the conversations he decided to go to the coffee shop daily so that he could establish a network with business men who go to the coffee shop for their business discussions.

It is said that one's network determines their next work, and their next work also determines their next wealth. As an entrepreneur, you should always be curious and develop the habit of asking people for their opinions about the things you do not understand. The more you ask, the more you will hear reasonable solutions to your problems. My friend discovered that people go to the coffee shop for much more than coffee. They have business discussions, study, or have meetings.

There was one particular person my friend always saw in the coffee shop. At first, my friend thought the man might have been the owner, because he dressed like an executive.

One day, my dear friend inquired about his background and wondered if the man could share his personal experience. As fate would have it, this man in a nice business suit, was going through a similar situation. However, his situation was slightly different.

He had lost his job and wanted to start something on his own, but did not have enough capital to rent an office apartment. The man spotted the coffee shop and thought it could be his partial office. He would invite people for a coffee with the main intention of discussing business. "I am doing well here and very soon, I will be able to move out to rent an official office space," he said.

That short conversation motivated my friend to also get started operating from the coffee shop, and using it as an office.

In the beginning, it was not easy, but in life as Jean de La Fontaine, French poet, once said "There is no road of flowers leading to glory."

My friend, used the coffee shop as his hub of operations for about two and a half years. He frequently arranged meetings with peers and prospective clients to discuss business. He was even able to reconnect with his former customers and added more. My friend even used the coffee shop for personal and professional development. While there, he took an online MBA course in order to improve his managerial skills.

Remember when I said, "Identify your main problem, and find a lasting solution to it?" This is exactly what my friend did. If you do this, you will move forward in your vision. My dear friend did not fail because there was no capital to start a business. He failed because he did not have enough managerial skills to manage, and to grow his established business.

Identify your weakness and find a lasting solution to it. That is the only way you could become successful in whatever it is that you are doing or intend to do.

CHAPTER 5
The Advice

It is said that there is no tree that the wind has not shaken. In other words, there is no single individual who has not gone through life challenges. And when we encounter challenges, at times all we can do is complain. But those who tend to give up their vision due to the challenges they face, have not yet realized that challenges are *part* of life. And that at every stage in our lives, we encounter different obstacles.

These challenges, obstacles, or struggles, should make us better, not bitter. They help us to know our strengths and weaknesses. Without challenges we would not be in a better position to measure our successes and failures in whatever we are doing. Nevertheless, the moment we quit we become failures.

A good friend of mine told to me that he never knew that the world had so many blessings for him until he was hit with serious challenges that made him move out of his shell (comfort zone). He remarked that initially, when confronted with problems, all the pressure would end his life.

Nonetheless, he decided to do something radical. This man stood up courageously to face the obstacles that were before him and overcame them. He later realized that those challenges were actually blessings in disguise.

This story reminds me of what Ernest Hemingway, great American novelist, once said, "Courage is grace under pressure."

My friend lost his job one month after his wife delivered their first baby. At a time when he needed more stability than at any other point in his life, he found himself without a source of income. In addition to this, his wife did not have a natural labor. She delivered in the seventh month. The cost of the cesarean operation had drained almost all of their savings and the baby was still in the incubator.

It seemed everywhere he turned there were more financial challenges. How could he handle this situation?

"My rent was also due," he said. "And my landlord was the type of person who would not even entertain being late on rent even a single day. Every time, I took a loan from my company to settle the rent, that amount was deducted from my salary the subsequent months. Now, I have lost my job. Oh, God! Why this time?" He lamented.

To cut a long story short, my friend ending up staying at home for almost a year and a half before he secured a new job. During this time, he was borrowing from family and friends to survive. - but he never gave up. He applied for other employment to about thirty different companies before he was hired. He looks back now and knows the challenges he went through were actually blessings in a disguise.

Today, he works for one of the biggest companies in his country, and just a year earlier, my friend was jobless and without hope. The salary is lucrative - much higher than his first position. As luck would have it, the company provided him with a house and a car. Now, life for him is comfortable, and he is finally in a better position to give back to the community.

Sometimes the challenges we go through gives us the tools we need to achieve our goals. A Chinese proverb says, "The gem cannot be polished without friction, nor man perfected without trials."

Those words illustrate that we only become "perfect (well close to perfect)" in what we are doing when we are able to overcome challenges. Unfortunately, many people have completely given up on their vision due to the fact that they could not withstand the challenges they faced.

Jim Rohn, American entrepreneur, author, and motivational speaker, once said, "Whatever good things we build, end up building us."

Therefore, you must choose to build up a strong attitude and a winner's mindset in order to face any problem that you may encounter. Don't let the situation you find yourself in now deter you from pursuing your goals because no condition is permanent.

As you push forward, you will be able to overcome your negative circumstance, and once that is done nothing can stop you from succeeding in life!

Always remember that life is a like a cup of coffee. You can always change it to suit your taste. Never give up. The moment you do, you become a failure.

It is my prayer that just as you have easily read this book so will your dreams and aspirations come true. I am very confident that if you put all that you have read here into practice, your life will never be as it once was. There are those who will only read this book, but will not bother to practice what this book is about.

I sincerely hope you are not one of them.

Acknowledgements

First, glory be to God for my life. I also wish to acknowledge with unique thanks, the assistance of those who have helpfully provided their time and support making this publication achievable. I'd like to make special mention of my parents, Nana Zacharia Appiah (Father), Abenaa Fati Yeboah (Mother), my wife Chen Wen, and my daughter Yebuwa Kuan, for their inspiration.

My special gratitude is extended to Mr. Siisi Osiban Nyampong for his support. Mr. Siisi Osiban Nyampong completed GCE O' Levels in Kadjebi-Asato Secondary School in the Volta Region of Ghana. He further went to the Institute of Management Studies in Accra where he earned a scholarship to study at Cambridge University in the United Kingdom for a Bachelor's Degree. In 1996, he graduated with BCom (Hons in Marketing). Mr. Nyampong became a Member of the Chartered Institute of Marketing in Ghana, 1997. He performed National Service with VRA Marine and upon completion, he was nominated as a Senior Marketing Officer with VLTC (Accra Branch Office) in VRA Headquarters. In 1998, Mr. Nyampong joined Mubarak Marine LLC in Dubai, where he conducted the relay communication for the first Humanitarian Supplies and Passenger Voyage to Umm Qasr and Bagdhad in Iraq in 2000 under the supervision of UN Oil for Food and Medicine Programmed.

In 2001, he completed the Seafarers' course at the Ghana Maritime Academy, and in 2004 he joined IAL Container Lines as Salesman and later was promoted to Branch Manager at Deira Branch Office in Dubai. During this time, he took correspondence studies of photojournalism covering the Persian Gulf and Arabian seas as well as the Bay of Bengal. Mr. Nyampong was transferred to Hong Kong in 2008 on a mission to research the possible establishments of branch offices in Japan, Thailand, and Mainland China. In 2010, he officially resigned from IAL Container Lines and Joined PWC in Shenzhen-China. Mr. Nyampong is now a private consultant and a managing partner of **SIDAGE CONSULTANCY AND MARKETING COMPANY LIMITED** and **AGROMINSTER COMPANY LIMITED**.

Also, special thanks are extended to Mr. Joshua Kojo Nkrumah for his encouragement. Mr. Nkrumah is a managing partner of Beijing Shiji Yingcai International Education Consulting Company ltd. Mr. Nkrumah is an educationalist and has about fifteen (15) years of experience as a teacher for both English Language and Mathematics. He also writes storybooks for children which are mostly embedded in the App called "English Tongue". Mr. Nkrumah holds a master's degree in Education.

I further acknowledge H.E. Dr. Denis G. Antoine for his review, comments, and recommendation for the improvement of this work.

H.E. Dr. Denis G. Antoine is the former Ambassador Extraordinary and Plenipotentiary of Grenada to the People's Republic of China from January 2016-2019. His functions included the full responsibilities for maintaining effective bilateral diplomatic relationship between the PRC and Grenada; and promotion of his country's interest within the community of nations represented in China and neighboring countries.

He is the Former Ambassador/Permanent Representative of Grenada to the United Nations from 2013 to 2015. Ambassador Antoine was elected and served as Vice President of the United Nations General Assembly for the 69th Session.

Before being appointed to serve at United Nations, Ambassador Antoine was Ambassador-At-Large and Director of the Office of International Programs and Exchange at University of the District of Columbia in Washington, D.C from 2009 to 2013.

During his tenure at the University, the Ambassador engaged in the conduct of Education Diplomacy, which included leading high-level delegations to countries such as Thailand, India, Egypt, China, Nigeria, Liberia, Ghana, Equatorial Guinea, London, and Sunderland in The United Kingdom. He worked closely with the Embassies of the Golf States, and other diplomatic Missions in Washington, D.C to promote negotiate and sign cooperation agreements with institutions of higher education, and conduct educational seminars.

Ambassador Antoine has served as Senior Election Observer with the Organization of American States (OAS), on missions to Guyana, Jamaica, and Commonwealth Dominica.

When he demitted Office in 2009, he was the second highest-ranking ambassador to the United States in Washington D.C. As one of the longest-serving ambassadors for his country, H.E Denis G. Antoine served as Grenada's Ambassador to the United States of America and Permanent Representative to the Organization of American States (OAS) in Washington, D.C and non-resident Ambassador for Grenada to Mexico and Panama concurrently, from 1995 to 2009.

He was Education Coordinator for Catholic Charities, Model Cities, in Washington, D.C from 1993-1994 and Education Supervisor for the District of Columbia Public Schools until 1995. Before his appointment as Ambassador of Grenada to the United States, Denis G. Antoine served as Program Specialist - Service Facility Regulator Department of Consumer and Regulatory Affairs for the Government of the District of Columbia from 1990 – 1992.

Ambassador Antoine has more than twenty (20) years of high level bilateral diplomatic experience in the United States, Mexico and Panama, the Inter-American System, and globally, which began when he served as Deputy Head of Mission and Counsellor/Alternate Representative to the OAS at the Embassy of Grenada in Washington, D.C, and as Charge d'Affairs during the period of May 1985 to December 1990.

He is the 2008 recipient of the Martin Luther King Jr. Legacy Award for International Service, he was the former Dean of the Corps of Ambassadors of the Western Hemisphere, and the Vice Dean of all ambassadors represented in the United States. He represented Grenada on the Board of Directors of the Inter-American Agency for Cooperation and Development (IACD) and served as Chairman of the Board of Directors of the Young Americas Business Trust, an affiliate of the OAS that works on youth and entrepreneurship in the Americas, and other charitable foundations.

Publications include "Get on Board Children of the World" 2020; "Effective Diplomacy in the Twenty-First Century: 2020; "Why is Everybody Looking at Me" in 2019 and a contribution to UN-HABITAT CSU Public Spaces for Sustainable Urbanization published by Talal Abu-Ghazaleh & Co. International in November 2016. In 2012, he published "Voice of Representation" a collection of letters, messages, and speeches of an ambassador and in 2009 he published a book "Effective Diplomacy – A Practitioners Guide" shares his insights on applied diplomacy in The United States of America and beyond.

About the Author

Awudu Quan, is the Chief Executive Officer of Beijing Mingyue Business Co., Ltd, and a managing partner of Quan Awudu Limited, and Maasikat Limited. Mr. Quan is also a successful Ghanaian writer, entrepreneur, businessman, and aspiring legal practitioner. Mr. Quan is the President of the Ghanaian Community Association in the China, Beijing Chapter. In addition to this, Mr. Quan has initiated several programs to promote investment opportunities in Africa and the Caribbean.

www.ingramcontent.com/pod-product-compliance
Lightning Source LLC
Chambersburg PA
CBHW071918070526
44583CB00016B/2039